A Bangladeshi's Tale

Amana Azim

BookLeaf Publishing

India | USA | UK

Presentation by *BookLeaf Publishing*

Web: www.bookleafpub.com

E-mail: info@bookleafpub.com

ISBN: 9789395969512

First edition 2023

DEDICATION

As mum would say,

Form your own identity and personality as that shows the world the real you.

ACKNOWLEDGEMENT

Assalamu alaykum. To the readers, thank you for giving these poems the love that I had while creating them. It truly feels unreal to be able to put my stories in a book when I have seen countless other readers do so, and now I get to do that too. To Allah (SWT), I am grateful that I even got this opportunity to do this, and inshallah, it touches the hearts of many. To the BookLeaf Publishing Team, sharing my Bangladeshi culture and Islamic faith throughout my poems has been the utmost special and raw experience that I wanted to share with the world. Thank you for making my wishes and dreams come true and that I can hold physically in my hands the work I have created.

To my mummy, the backbone of my life, my guardian angel, nothing I do is without you. I remember you telling me to write a book about all the annoying things I and my siblings do to you, and it would be a best-selling book. I laughed, but here we are. The experiences you have faced inspired me to write this book. I love you.

To baba, thank you for encouraging me that I can do it, and now know that I have what it takes. I love you.

To my worlds: Amera and Zayed, there is not one second in me that I feel that I do not feel for you and love you as much. I always think of ways to be there for you both. I love you both with my whole heart and thank you both for making the best memories with me together. Growing up, you both were the sunshine of my life, and I could not have been more grateful to have you both as my siblings and to play the most fun games together. Part of my poems reflect the memories we have made, and I am so happy that I am able to do this for you both, alhamdulillah.

To all the people that share the love of books love books and bookstagrammers and booktokers, thank you for getting me back into reading and realizing the craft of stories, and for getting me back into reading, thank you.

To Bangladesh: my country, a heart of gold, the experiences and memories I have there are ones I always cherish the most, can't wait till the next time I go back to visit there.

To Melbourne: I can't wait to make more memories in this city, here's to reaching new heights and beyond and catching our dreams.

Mum

They say paradise lies under the mother's feet.
I never knew what it meant till I was older.
Their unconditional love for their children is the
most purest form of love.
You never find anywhere else.
The unnoticed sacrifices that I never knew when
I was little how hard it is to do.
But once I was older, I realised that she made
those choices for us.
For a better future for us.
I will always be grateful for you mummy.
For all the times you have helped me with my
homework.
For all the times you have stayed up all night
holding us in your arms making sure that we are
looked after and cared for. Even though you
really needed some sleep.
For all the times when life was unpredictable
you never fought a battle without a fight.
Your love was always there for your little son
and twin daughters.
For us your love was there forever.
And inshallah, I am able to give you the
happiness you deserve and be the light of your
life.
I love you more and more everyday.

Baba

To the person who has worked day and night for
us.
who studied abroad and built a better future for
us
by coming to a whole new country with mum
and starting all over again
everything new and unknown.
It was tough but you worked your way up.
and then there were your two daughters, the joys
of your life.
growing up together in front of you
the angels walking around the house picking
flowers from the garden and helping you plant
vegetables in the garden
going on walks together and trips together were
so much fun
I love you for all the sacrifices that you have
done and continue to do everyday baba.

Bon and Bhai

To my bon.
Inseparable since birth.
3 months earlier than expected, I could have lost
you or you could have lost me.
But we made it together with mummy and baba
alhamdulillah.
We shared the best memories together
my favourite being the matching outfits which
stayed with us till we were older, moving on to
having the perfect hijab shades to match our
outfits too. Dressing up is our favourite thing
and I would not have wanted it any other way
with any other person.
I love you, my twin sister.
To my brother.
you were the joy when you were born.
I would not have wanted a bigger blessing than
you.
From your smile and playful energy that lights
up my world and everyone else around you
Thank you for changing our lives.
I love you, little bhai.

A dreamy night

We walk down the streets together
hand in hand
The white dress against my skin was shining in the
sunlight
the summer breeze dancing the cotton fabric around
in swirls the cool linen helping me stay cool during
the breeze
as we walk down under the lights I spot jasmine
flower bracelets
sitting there oh so dainty
as I walk towards the trolley I smell them
the fragrance smelling like the sweet floral scent I
have always known them for
I get two and put them on my hands
The perfume of them surrounding me
I smile and get shy as they match my dress perfectly
and compliment my outfit making me feel like a
princess
we walk a bit more and see a garden

A garden filled with flowers
red and pink bursts surrounded the trees
we take in our surroundings looking at the beautiful
garden around us
I soak in the beauty of it all as much as my eyes
could see
I felt a small jasmine flower on my hijab

and I smiled another foolish smile and felt my cheeks
blush.
the chaand shined upon us
making this a dreamy night

Chaand

The chaand shined upon the streets
glowing in the night sky
it never fails to stop shining
on the people who look up to it every night
as I lay my head on my bed
I stare at the moon
a smile rises on my face as I fall asleep
looking at Allah's creation and being
mesmerised by the beauty of it

Hometown

As I board the plane with my luggage in my
hand I cannot contain my excitement
the boarding announcement announcing our
gates open makes me jumping like a little child
with candy
because I knew in 10 hours we will be reaching
home
Our home country
Our desh
Bangladesh
The flight was cozy the way I always knew
flying on an aeroplane was my favourite
As the flight was ready for take-off I closed my
eyes
hearing the blast of the engine turning I knew we
were going to take off anytime soon
the wheels start moving and we start moving too
then it moves faster
and
faster
then before we knew it we were up in there and
high in the clouds
the clouds so soft that I could reach them with
my hands

the happiness and excitement danced around in
my belly
my eyes widening in delight at the view
hours passed by
I had a yummy meal and my stomach was full
I closed my eyes as the lights went out for a nap
time
I kept dreaming about the time we would land in
Bangladesh
and before I knew it we were here
in Chittagong Bangladesh
Home at last

Journey

Some days you would seem that everything in
life is hard
some days you would be struggling to get
through
Sometimes you'll feel like you're dreaming too
hard and that your dream is out of reach.
But all that takes is changing the way you view
things in life.
Change the I can't to I can
The no I am not good at this to I'll try my
hardest
From thinking of giving up to having the drive
to succeed. The I give up to I will do this and
succeed.
As you reach the end of your goal
You'll look back and realise it was meant to be
Not in the way you might have imagined but
you're here. The end result will be sweet, but the
journey to get there and reflect is sweeter.

Prayer

As the azaan goes on, I hear the words.
I feel the calmness go over me once I hear them
I walk towards the place to pray
the mosque oh so beautiful
I see others going to the same place as I am
Subhanallah we all gather at the same place at
the same time
all together to gather in doing the same actions
together.
to pray together, to unite together

Blessings

As I sit down on my prayer mat, the softness of
the mat makes me feel warm.
the simple action of reciting the prayers
I put my hands together and say the words
I feel blessed that I have this opportunity
to thank Allah my creator of all the things I was
given
food, shelter, family which many might not have
but I was given the opportunity to thank him for
all the things he has given me

.

Taraweeh

It is Ramadan Night.
Iftar was a scrumptious delight filled with all our
favourite foods
It was nearly Taraweeh time
we step inside the masjid and see hundreds of
people lined up
we put our shoes on the racks and step inside
I see everyone being prepared in getting ready
for prayer
20 rakahs was long
but that is what is special about it
the prayers that are special on this month than
any other month is that it is longer
I smile knowing that it is the month of blessings
Knowing that I'll get seventy more blessings
makes me feel at ease.
As we start our prayer, I feel grateful and happy
that I have the opportunity of life to witness this
special month again.

Ramadan

The twinkling lights shine around you
the breeze feeling cool
the feeling of blessings showering upon you
the adrenaline rush of finding the moon in the
sky
we spot the moon shining in the night glistening
in the light
Now we know it is the first day of Ramadan.
I went to the first Taraweeh prayer.
When I finished, I had my tasbih around my
hands saying the names of Allah and prayers.
This was Ramadan I wanted to be a better
Muslim.
A change in me where I feel fulfilled about what
I have achieved.
The feeling that when I return to him, that I
know in this Dunya, I have done something that
will lead me to Jannah inshallah.
Knowing that I have made a change in
someone's life through my prayers and actions.

Chaand Raat

It is the last day of Ramadan.
you prayed the last Taraweeh yesterday and the
masjid was filled with people praying their final
Taraweeh salah. Trying to make the most good
deeds out of the blessed month that passed by.
You get home and see mum making sweets for
eid tomorrow.
The sugar, the milk, the cinnamon and the
pistachios all mixed up to make rasmalai and
gulab jamun.
You get ready in your salwar kameez and slide
on your silver churis down your hand
glimmering in the light Then you go sit with the
girls chattering away in the living room, filling
the atmosphere with festive celebratory vibes
gathering around as you all wait to put on
mehendi together.
Under the twinkly light and the Eid Mubarak
sign, we get our mehendi designs ready.
From florals to intricate leaf patterns and swirls
our hands are covered in beautiful designs of art.
I cannot stop smiling as I look at my hands
covered in the beautiful mehendi, hoping it
stains red when I wake up tomorrow.

As I wash the stain and let my mehendi dry. I have a smile on my face as I go back to bed knowing how much mehendi makes me happy and the cultural meaning behind it.
I hope that Eid day goes well tomorrow, just as magical as it always is inshallah.

Eid

It was the morning of what I was waiting for the whole year. Eid day.
I wake up feeling as excited as ever.
And then I see my hands.
My mehendi was red in colour and the stain showcased all the floral patterns so beautifully placed on my hand.
I stared at it in awe and how beautiful my hands looked and squealed in delight.
As I went to my mum's room I hugged her and said, Eid Mubarak.
she replied with Eid Mubarak to you too.
Then I went to go shower and put on my eid clothes.
The beautiful salwar kameez looked absolutely perfect.
just the way I imagined it.
As I put on my hijab and makeup I was excited to put on my jewellery and accessorise my outfit.
With a tikli on my forehead and churi's on my wrists I looked at myself in the mirror.
I looked like a princess.
As I stepped out to wear my Nagra shoes to finish my look, mum came out and looked at me.

That look made me feel like the prettiest girl in
the world.
and I did feel like I was the prettiest girl in the
world.
I tasted the firni and shemai that I always have
for Eid breakfast and it was sweet and delicious,
just perfect the way mum always makes it.
I couldn't wait to see all my cousins because I
knew that this day was going to be the most
special day ever.

Laal Saree

The Laal saree
a classic Bangladeshi favourite
six yards of pure grace as I laid my eyes upon it in
my mummy's saree collection.
The red jamdani cloth stared at me and my eyes
widened in awe
at how beautiful traditional clothes are
my mum got the saree out of the bag
and helped me put it on
she got her pins and helped pin them on
creating wraps and pleats oh so perfect
I was mesmerised by her talent
the way she drapes a saree so beautifully it felt like
watching an artist create art.
once she secures the final pins she looks at me
she starts getting teary
and I get teary watching her
I feel special wearing her saree
I knew I will look like my mum in it
because she is the prettiest woman I knew, mashallah
I look up and walk towards the mirror and I was not
wrong
mum, laal jamdani saree is beautiful
it made me look like the most beautiful woman in the
entire world

Beach

You lay down on your cool linen blanket.
feeling the sand in between your toes tickling
you.
You have a nice drink of fresh orange juice just
by your side.
A drink that reminds you of the sweetness of life
and all the good things it has to offer.
You hear the waves crashing by as you look up
from reading your favourite book.
you have a big smile on your face at what you
see.
families playing volleyball in the sand.
little children building sandcastles by filling
their tiny buckets
other little children collecting seashells and
trying to find the most unique one.
and the others enjoying swimming in the waves
of the ocean splashing each other with water.
You see people sipping their coconut water
enjoying their refreshing drink by the sunset.
As you watch everyone enjoy themselves at the
beach including you, you realise this is what life
is about. Doing the little joys that make you
happy and make you live life to the fullest.

Pohela Boishakh

As we wake up to the sound of the parade from
the streets, my cousins and I rush towards the
window.
Masks and costumes were worn by hundreds of
people down the street.
We see the colourful flags of red, green and
white down the streets filling the community
with colour.
We are excited that we will be enjoying the
parade with everyone else.
I get ready in our white and red salwar kameez
and my brothers in a white kurta.
We go out on the streets filled with colour.
We go out to have our favourite foods.
Hot jilapi was sizzling in the oil and getting
soaked in the sugar syrup. I could feel and taste
the sweetness of it. My favourite Bangladeshi
sweet ever.
Fuchka was next.
Me and the brothers compete to see who can
have the most.
The soft and spicy chotpoti dancing in my
mouth.

With a bite of the fuchka shell and the tetul
sauce it was a match made in heaven.
As the night settles in, the lights of the cha tea
shop glimmer in delight making the space warm
and inviting.
We sit on the stools in the little cha shop near
our house.
Then we have gorom cha and pita.
The perfect sweet combo.
I drink the cha and it tastes so sweet.
The pita, soft and fluffy that melts in your
mouth.
We all laugh and share stories together while
having our cha and pita.
As we do, I realise how these moments are the
ones I'll remember forever.

A Bangladeshi Iftar

The time to break our fast is near.
We could hear the little grumbles of our stomachs
wanting the delicious food.
The piyaju's frying in the oil till they are crispy
golden brown.
The dates have been placed in the centre of the table
because there is no iftar complete without it.
The beguni sitting on the table waiting to hear the
perfect crunch of the batter, knowing that the crunch
is the key for it to be perfect.
The lebu shorbot was stirred in the jug with ice
knowing that it is everyone's favourite drink.
The haleem, warm and cosy like a homemade
heartfelt meal that would hug you back with cuddles.
That is what that tastes like.
A comfort meal.

Of course, there is no meal without something sweet.
My favourite rasmalai, decorated with rose petals and
pistachios, what's not to love? A homemade cake, my
favourite kind.
With strawberries, chocolate and cream, what's not to
love?
As the azaan plays, we reach our hands together in
prayer to make a dua.
I made one, a special one that is close to my heart.

To always be surrounded by my loved ones and
family.
And that I am grateful that they are all around me
today here, on this special time during Ramadan.

Spring

The weather is getting warmer
From those cold winter days and nights to the
sun peaking through the clouds
The trees start to get their life back
As you see the green leaves growing back on
them
You see the flowers starting to grow
the bursts of colour bringing you joy and delight
From yellow to pink to purple and blue
It is like a rainbow of colours surrounding the
front yards of each house as you walk down the
neighbourhood.
With a light cardigan over your kurti, you finally
feel the season
the time to soak all the positive energy and
sunshine there is around you.
you twirl around the flower trees and feel like
the happiest girl ever.